Happy Birthday to _____ !

# Color With Me!

## Grandma & Me
## Birthday Party
## Animals

Sandy Mahony
Mary Lou Brown

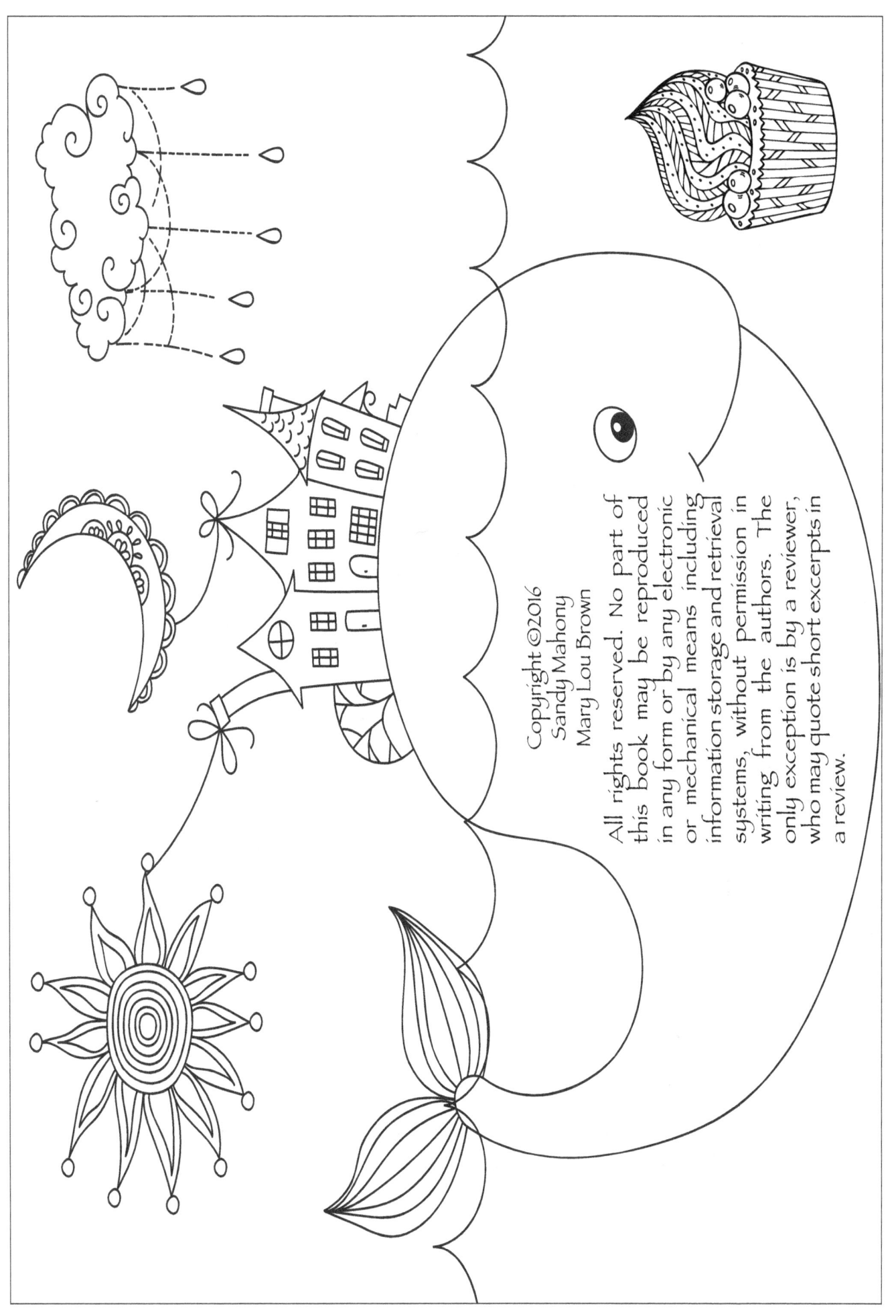

The animals have sent out the party invitations!

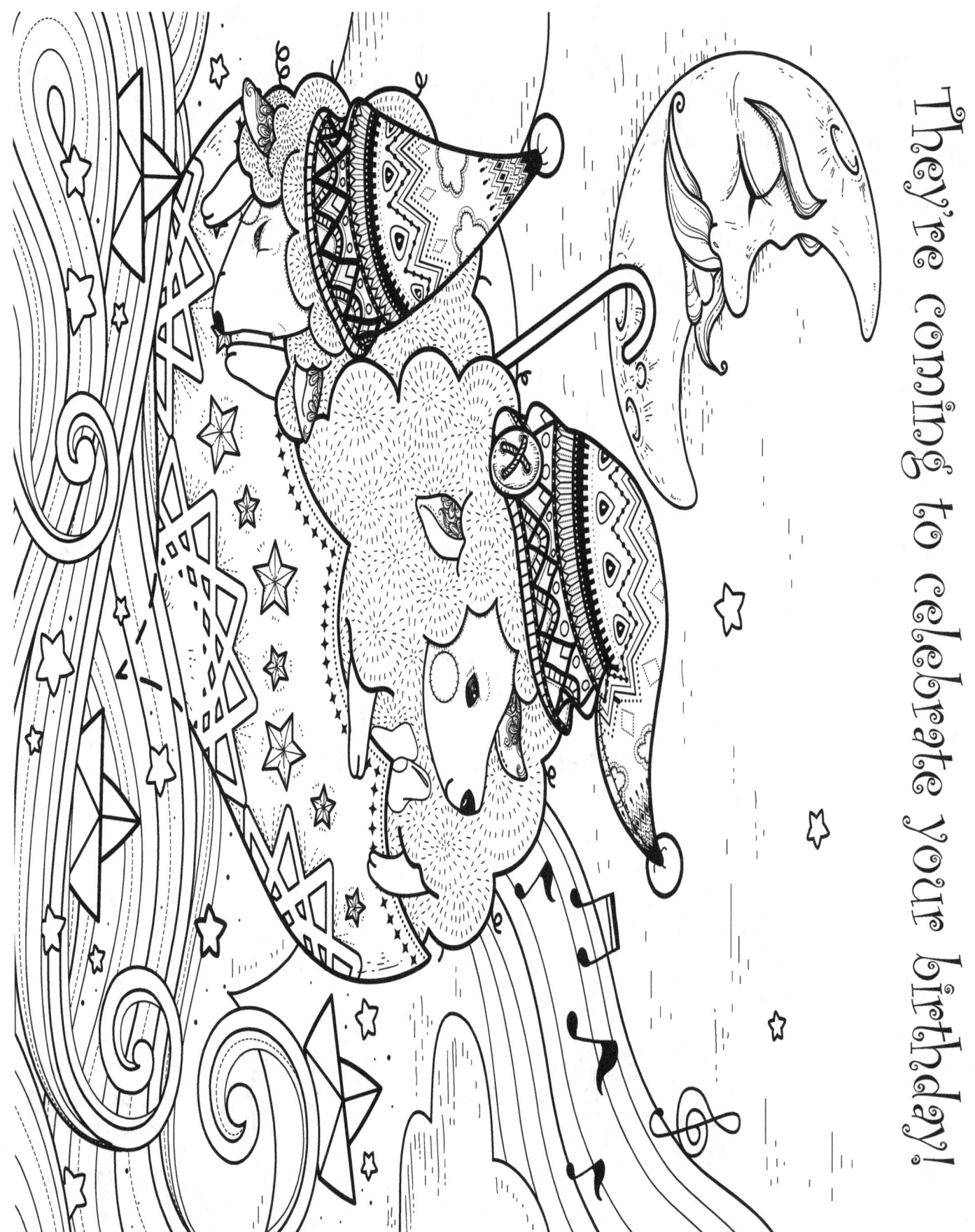

They're coming to celebrate your birthday!

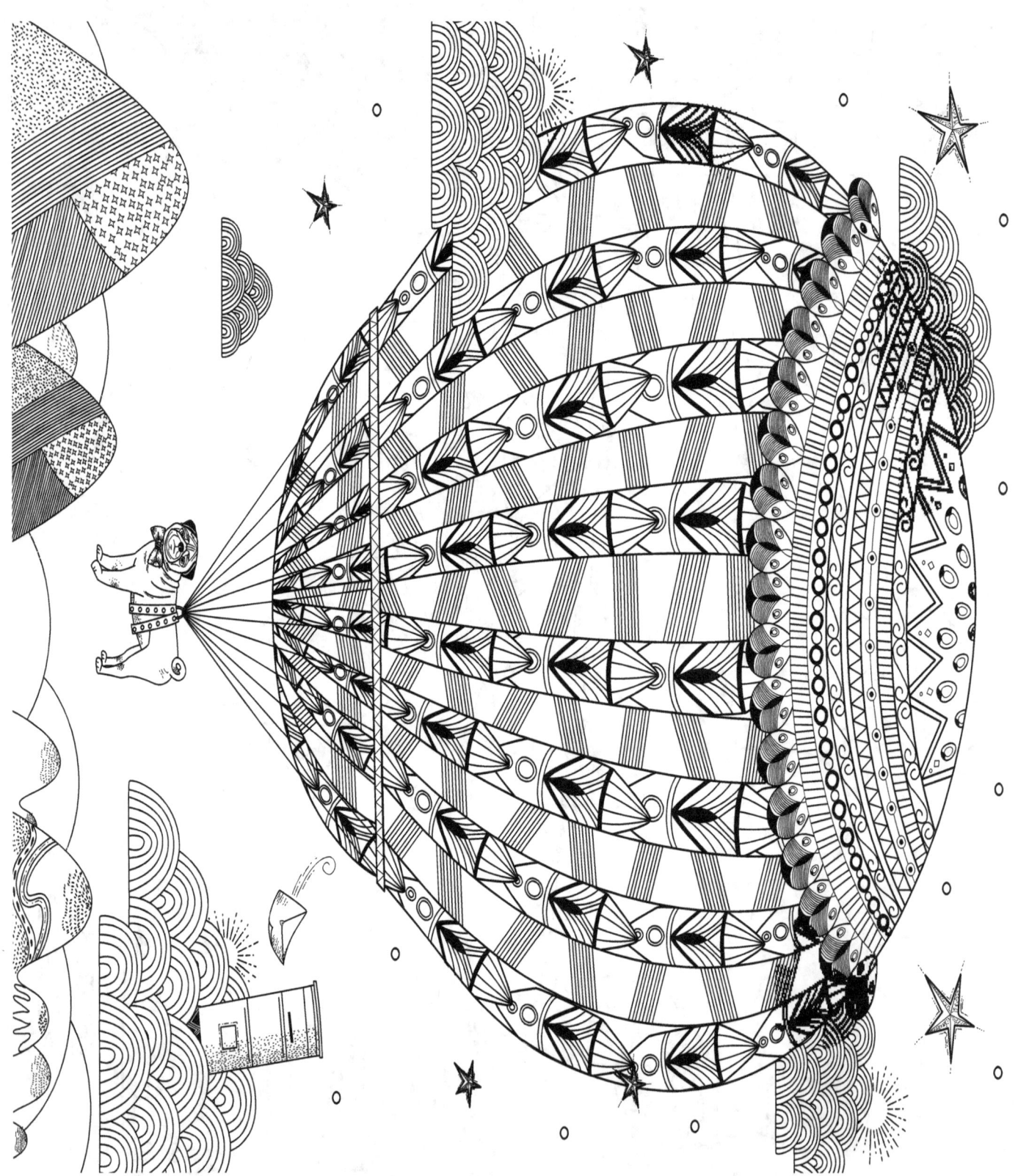

Let's get this party started!

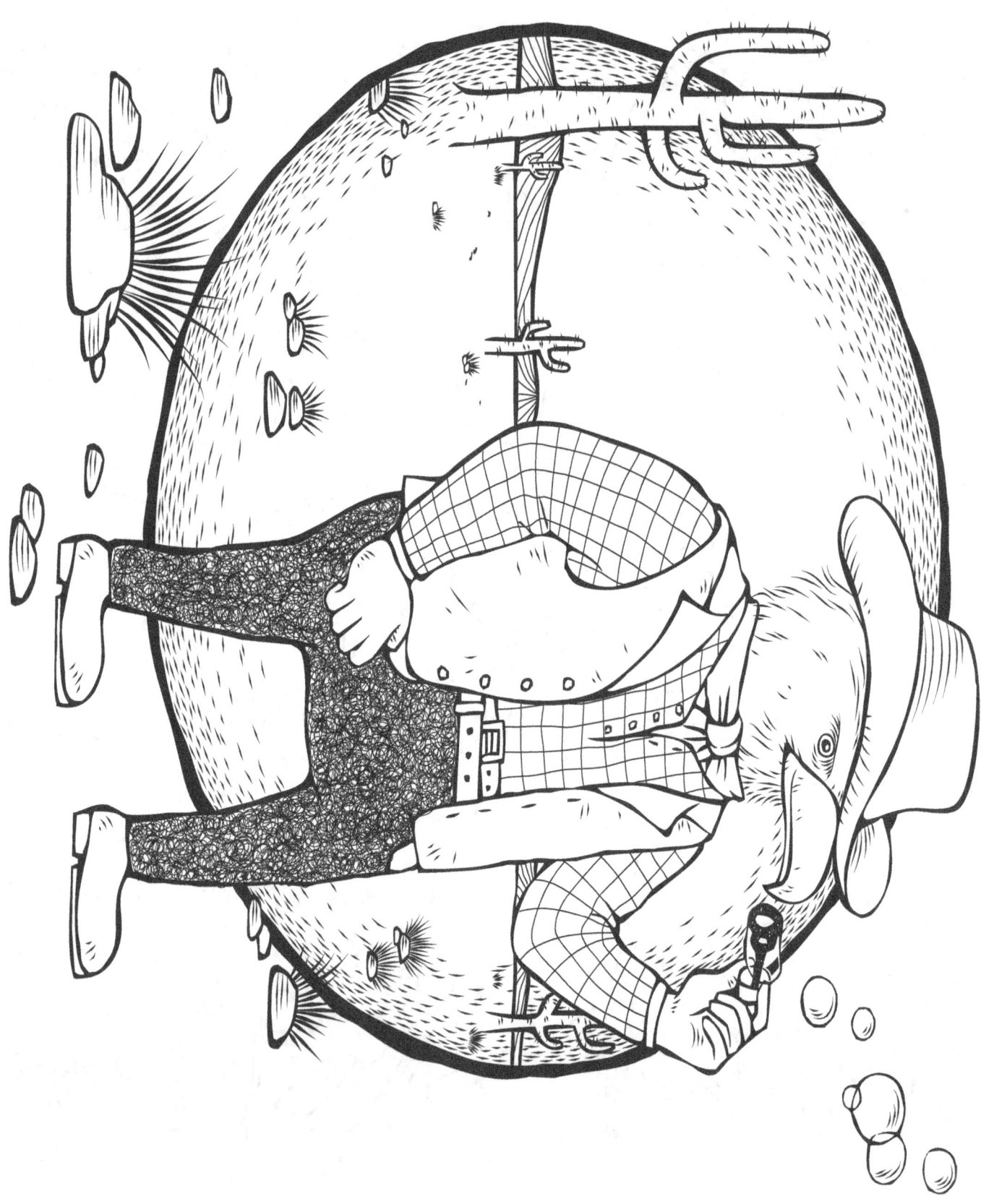

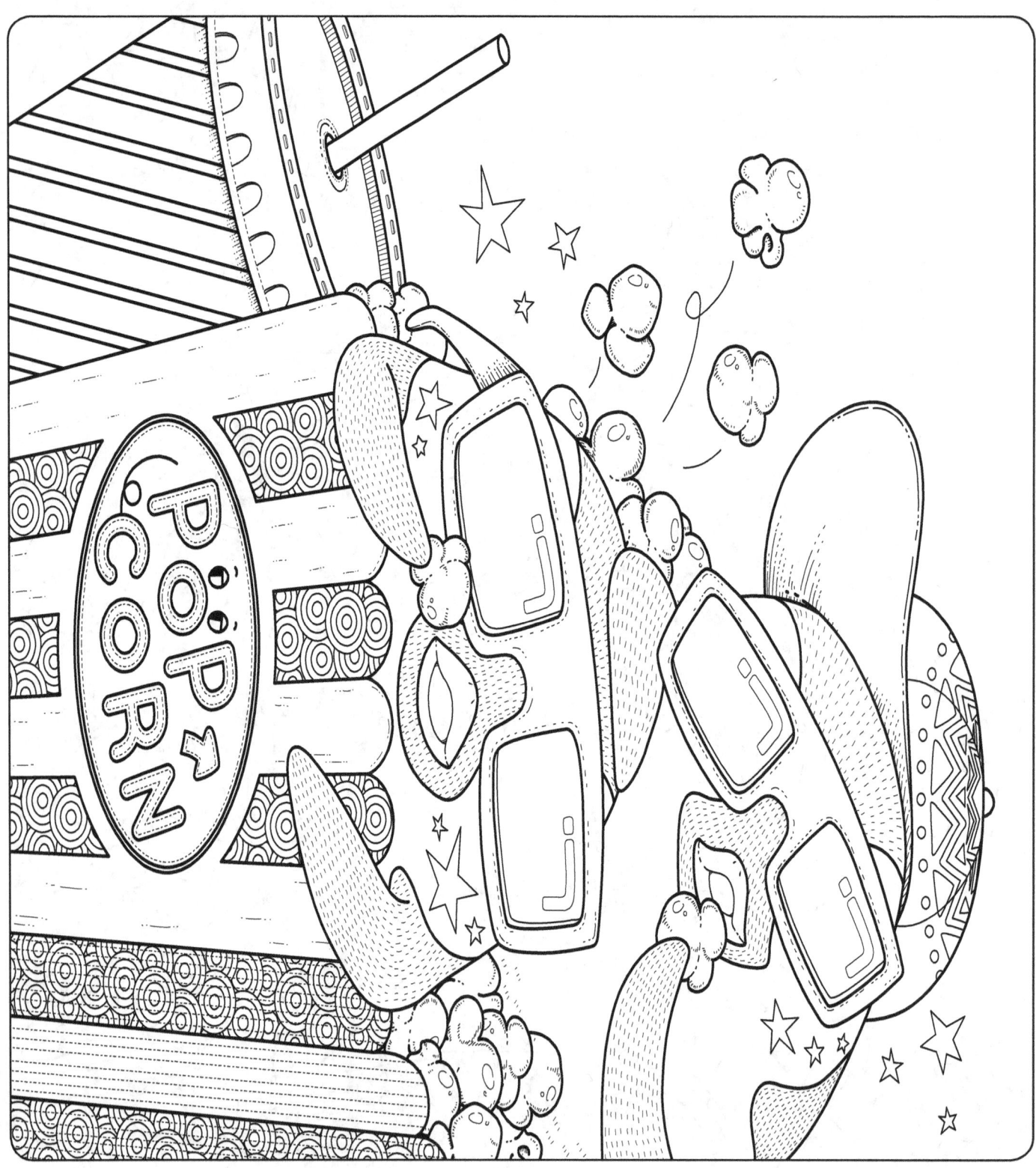

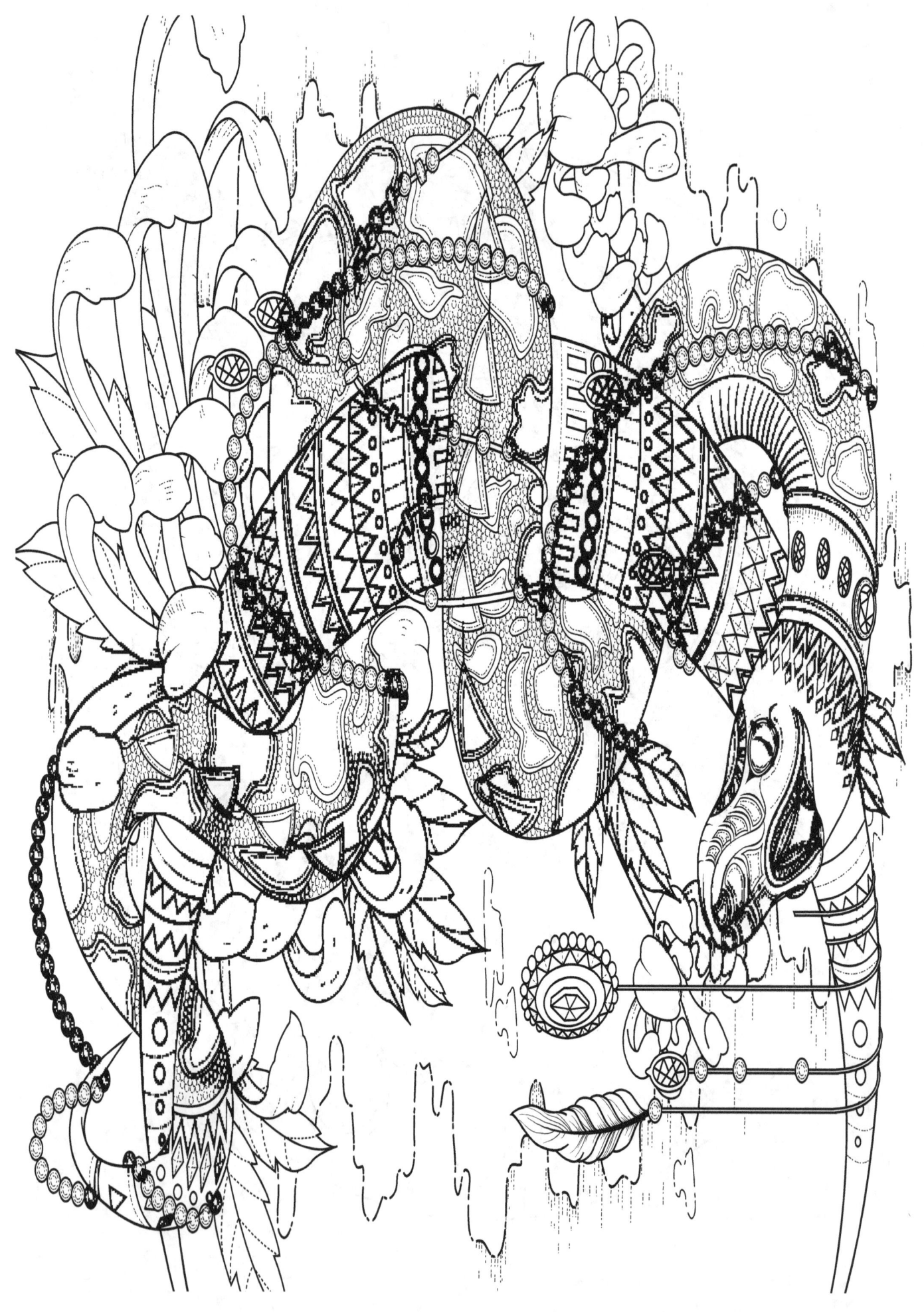

DON'T·FORGET·TO·SMILE·

Happy Birthday!